.

A PARENT HANDBOOK FOR SCHOOL AGE CHILDREN WITH LEARNING DISABILITIES

IDEA 2004
Individuals with Disabilities Education Improvement Act

By Shelley Smith

authorHOUSE™

1663 LIBERTY DRIVE, SUITE 200
BLOOMINGTON, INDIANA 47403
(800) 839-8640
WWW.AUTHORHOUSE.COM

First published by AuthorHouse 12/20/05

ISBN: 1-4259-0630-3 (sc)

Library of Congress Control Number: 2005910735

Printed in the United States of America
Bloomington, Indiana

This book is printed on acid-free paper.

*This book is dedicated to
my wonderful husband,
amazing children,
and our family.*

*"I need someone to tell me what to say!" For me -
just talking to you gave me a lot more confidence
in what I was doing. And it's that back-up and
support that most parents don't get. One of the
books I read talked about how when you walk in
the door to a school - suddenly you are 10 years
old and the principal is looming above you like
you were a kid again. I think remembering
the fact that you are on the same playing field
as they are - and you have the experience and
training necessary is one of the key issues!"*

**Parent of child with special needs*

Thank you to family, friends, and colleagues for reading my manuscript and providing helpful critiques. Best wishes and heartfelt thanks to:

My wonderful parents Bill and Penny

My sister Stacey

My brother Vic

Todd S.

Kim B.

Lynn A.

Kerry B.

Gwen B.

A special thanks to
Michelle B. and Cindy L.

NOTE TO READER

If you gain anything from this book, even if you don't read this book, remember this phrase, use this phrase, and repeat this phrase:

"I feel that you are violating my parental rights and in doing so you are also infringing upon my child's right to her federally mandated free and appropriate public education."

FOREWORD

"Please sign here that you have received your rights, and that you understand these rights as presented to you."

WHAT??!! My right to remain silent and confused by all that is presented to me? Anything I say may be used for future humiliation if I sound uninformed or illogical? I have the right to an attorney if and when mediation is unsuccessful, but good luck hiring one who truly understands the nuance of special education law? If I cannot afford an attorney, part but not all of my legal expenses may be reimbursed but only if I am successful in defending my child's special education rights?

For every parent of a child with special needs who has experienced the great puzzle that is "public education," who has sat across the table (or surrounded at the table) by the professionals who go on endlessly about our precious person's needs seldom focusing on positive aspects of his or her potential, this may seem eerily familiar. Maybe there is a reason that parents start to "accidentally forget" I.E.P. meetings or parent teacher conferences? Do schools no longer provide training in "couching" information when presenting to a parent? (Couching...a term loosely meaning that a professional start with a positive statement or story, insert the message of concern, and follow up with more positives creating a unified and supportive "team."). *Later we may visit the 5th grade band teacher who could for some unknown reason never deliver positive news. However, the nasty-grams were frequent and utilized extremely poor grammar which I found it necessary to correct and return to her. I don't recommend this method.* For those who have experienced this "great divide," may this be a useful guide in understanding and navigating the waters of the special education process.

I am a mother of a special needs child, sister of siblings with "special gifts," and daughter to ...shall we say...special people. I too, falling not far from the tree, struggle with otherwise-abled abilities. Unfortunately, my siblings and I lived in a time and place where our needs were not necessarily understood or dealt with. This being said, and being highly over-educated, I pursued my own child's special needs and rights with a vengeance. Not always, I might add, in his best interest. Let's just say for the record, I was not always terribly appreciated in my children's schools. *Later we may address the second grade teacher who accused me of stalking her classroom to, apparently, raid her plan book and ruin the class's surprise teddy bear party, time and editor permitting.* I could; however, draft and fire off a very realistic and researched brief that could get many an administrator jumping, again, not always necessarily in my child's best interest. Adding case law and legalistic jargon can be quite inciting when utilized appropriately!

"I think the thing that you can pass along better than anything else is your passion for kids that need somebody to care about what they need outside the system rather than how they simply need to fit into the system. Once somebody has the heart for kids that are different, they won't break any sort of law because they will be taking such good care of what makes their own life special. Admittedly, there are those that have no place in their heart for anything but what makes their life easier, less expensive and more fun and you'll have to find a way to corral them and teach them that it is easier to play the game than to grump about it........ GOOD LUCK!"

    ** *Commentary from a friend in response to the writing of A Parent Handbook*

Purpose and Goals

Having the "otherwise-abled abilities" that I have, I have jumped from the military, to medical microbiology, to medical technology, to school psychology, to a run at a PhD in special education law/systems enhancement leadership, to a stint on the school board, back to medical technology, and finally back to education (*for the moment*). During this frenetic, or as my husband might say...flaky, career path, I realized that my one true passion has remained child advocacy. Having volunteered as an advocate and advocating in the educational system, it made sense that I would make and effort to expand this reach. The intent of this project is to create a meaningful and useable resource for parents in advocating for their own child with special needs.

What Is In This Handbook?

The first chapter of the book is somewhat of an overview as to why I decided to try and write the book. It is a combination of personal and professional experience along with a brief overview of the history of the developing laws leading to the Individuals with Disabilities Educational Act of 2004. Chapter two provides an abbreviated look at why public education is so important in a democracy and how the governmental entities and social events influenced educational policy. Chapter three provides an overview of disability laws, which affect education, while chapter four provides more of an in-depth look at IDEA 2004. In chapter five I define and discuss some of the procedural safeguards and parent rights. Chapter six provides a somewhat detailed overview of discipline guidelines regarding a child in special education. Chapter seven explains Individual Education Programs. Chapter eight is an overview of the placement process into special education. In chapter nine we look at the "so what" factor of the book. I've now got this information so...what do I do with it? In chapter ten we look at "big brother" who is monitoring the state and local educational agencies.

Disclaimer

I am not an attorney and am not professing to express an official opinion. The book is intended to provide an overview with, hopefully, readable language to assist parents in his or her advocacy roles. It should not be construed as a legal text or comprehensive legal analysis of special education law. Nothing in the book should be considered legal advice. Parents should consult an attorney when significant legal questions arise.

CONTENTS

Chapter 4 19
SPED Law IDEA 2004

Chapter 5 29
You Decided What About My Child Without Me?

Chapter 9 69
Now What?!

Chapter 10 75
Federal Monitoring

"I wish I could express to you what a relief it was to talk to you last night. This battle with the schools has gone on for so many years that I am just beaten down and exhausted. Yesterday I didn't have an ounce of fight left in me after the meeting at school and (I) had pretty much given up on *Tim's education all together. It was so nice to talk to you and know that I am not crazy, not a horrible parent, and as I suspected - the school is doing wrong by my child! I immediately called the mother of the child that was supposed to be notified - and told her what you said - and she said, "I want to meet this woman and kiss her!" Can you hear me smiling?! My smile is going from ear to ear"!

** parent of child with autism

I feel that you are violating my parental rights and in doing so you are also infringing upon my child's right to her federally mandated free and appropriate public education.

Chapter 1

Sitting on the *Other* *Side* of the Table

Many of my colleagues do double duty as an educational professional as well as a parent, sometimes of a special needs child. I have often had the conversation regarding the seeming metamorphosis, which occurs when walking into your own child's I.E.P. meeting or Parent Teacher Conference. For some reason the doorway to the table becomes a myopic kaleidoscope filled journey, which grows longer with every step taken. A teacher or group of professionals wait at a table with all eyes turned towards you as you make this torturous trek. These people may even be people you work with daily; however, they are now an adversarial pack of wolves waiting to devour you with the latest update of calamity your child may have caused. For some reason the chairs they sit in seem to be of normal height; however, the one at the head of the table left thoughtfully for you, the parent, seems to be roughly that of a kindergarten chair leaving your knees at your chin and the table approximately even with your nose.

Help I am Surrounded!

I have often wondered what it must be like for a parent without the education background, knowledge, and experience to face this overwhelming situation. When my son was making the transition to high school we had the perfunctory I.E.P. transition meeting, which included high school representatives as well as our "sending" team. At the time I was a school board member, doctoral candidate in special education law/ systems enhancement leadership, school psychologist and rather ferociously protective mom. The high school "administrative representative" had the audacity to inform me that she could not and would not sign off on the accommodations section of the I.E.P. because it conflicted with "their policy." When I asked her for a copy of this policy, which evidently must be important enough to outrank federal policy (tongue in cheek), the person scowled at me and failed to produce said *policy*. A few weeks later I received a single sheet of paper outlining one teacher's class policy indicating that no late work would be accepted. Amazing! These "representatives" actually expected to be able to defy special education federal law, a civil rights mandate, due to a single teacher's feeble classroom rules policy. If they were willing to pull this stunt with me, how would a parent without a rather large mouth have advocated for his or her child?

The Parent Advocate

School can be a difficult place for any student regardless of race, socio-economic status, disability, or gender.

Advocating for a child with a teacher or school can be a daunting task for any parent. When a child has a disability, the experience can be exponentially greater. Some parents are upset about difficulties faced in advocating for their child. This can be a very trying situation. Understanding the law, navigating "the system," or questioning the professionals can leave a parent feeling overwhelmed and under qualified. Although it is generally an unspoken rule, many parents and professionals recognize that school districts often create the need to "do battle" for appropriate services, supports, and settings.

Every parent wants what is best for his or her child. The Education for All Handicapped Children Act (PL 94-142) enacted in 1975 was intended to support and protect children with special education needs. In order to receive federal funding, states were required to develop and put into place policies, which would assure a free and appropriate public education to all children. Unfortunately, special education law as with any law can be ambiguous, difficult to understand, and open to multiple interpretations. New avenues and protections were opened to children with disabilities, but parents and even professionals were left with little understanding of how to advocate effectively.

The Individual with Disabilities Education Act of 1997 further aspired to help everyone be competitive in today's global society by reaching his or her full potential through a free and appropriate public education. Some provisions and monies were allocated for parent training centers and other forms of support; however, many parents continued

3

to be baffled as to how to stand up for their child when all of the professionals seemed to have formed a preconceived opinion on placement or services. *Of course this was never done without the parents present...wink wink...as that would violate the intent of the law.*

The new authorization, which became effective in July 2005 called the Individual with Disabilities Education Improvement Act or IDEA 2004, allocates money for Parent Training and Information Centers. The reauthorization changes the original language of the act to include the partial statement, "strengthening the role and responsibility of parents and ensuring that families of such children have meaningful opportunities to participate in the education of their children at school and at home." The previous language did not include the words, *"and responsibility"* of parents. Clearly the intent of these laws includes having parents aware and actively involved in their child's education, but short of classes being provided in every school district by an expert in the area, it will remain a difficult situation at best. The best way for a parent to effectively advocate and be an informed collaborator in his or her child's education is to pursue knowledge on their own through the internet, books, courses, speakers, advocacy groups, and etc.

I feel that you are violating my parental rights and in doing so you are also infringing upon my child's right to her federally mandated free and appropriate public education.

Chapter 2
What is Public Education All About?

Although history lessons can be dry and even painful, the following is a brief overview of the basis of education in a successful democracy and a quick review of the federal government's involvement in education. An overall understanding of why we do things can be helpful in gaining a more broad perspective regarding special education today and assist us in our parental advocacy roles. *It is nice to be on the same footing as the professionals when discussing the subject!*

A Democratic Society

The American government and the society in which we live are based upon the concept of democracy. A strong democracy should be pervasive within all aspects of society and social life (MacPherson, 1977). Citizens of the United States enjoy civil and political rights as well as limited social and economic rights. Democracy as a concept for government first started with the Greeks, but was then "lost" for over 2,000 years. When the founding fathers of our country began trying to envision the best way for all to achieve full potential, democracy began to be embraced (Sullivan, 1995). However, democracy was originally thought of as "mob rule" where the poor, ignorant, and incompetent could make decisions at the expense of the property owners and leisured class. In order to nurture the fragile concept, which was difficult to develop and maintain, all Americans needed to understand the philosophical basis for democracy and how to support the process (MacPherson, 1977). Education helps to foster these democratic skills and virtues for collaboration with other citizens socially, politically, and economically (Harrison, 2003). Therefore, a free and appropriate public education may indeed be the true foundation for a democratic society.

Checks and Balances

Our democratic government is broken down into the Legislative, Executive, and Judicial branches. These branches are designed in a manner so as to keep each other in line through a process of checks and balances. The Legislative branch's job includes allocating funding and making laws. The Executive branch's job includes issuing and making sure that laws created by the Legislative branch are carried out. The Judicial branch is tasked with interpreting the laws created by the Legislative branch (Turnbull& Turnbull, 2000).

The Legislative branch at the Federal level includes the House of Representatives (Congress) and the Senate. At the state level, the legislative branch includes the State General

Assembly. Locally the Legislative branch includes the City Council and the Local School Board. The Executive branch at the Federal level includes the President of the United States and the Department of Education. At the state level, the Executive branch includes the State Governors. Locally, the Executive branch consists of the town Mayor, County Executive, and school Superintendents. The Judicial branch at the Federal level is represented as the United States Supreme Court. At the state level, are the State Supreme Courts. Lastly are the various local courts (Turnbull& Turnbull, 2000).

In Steps the Federal Government

Control over schools remained local until 1954 (Brown vs. Topeka Board of Education), when the courts ruled that separate was not equal in terms of the services and quality of education provided. After the Brown decision, Federal roles in education became more evident. In 1957 the National Defense Education Act was enacted as a response to Sputnik. The Act sponsored a return to the core curriculum in order to beef up in science and math especially as the Russians were seen to be gaining an advantage on the United States in the race to the moon and in the cold war. During the 1960's came a civil rights era spawning Head Start and vocational education programs. The Elementary and Secondary Education Act targeted low income, migrant, and non-English speaking children.

The 1970's extended the Civil Rights movement. In 1973, ESEA was amended to provide Federal funding to schools for educating students with disabilities. War issues contributed as well in part because veterans were coming back very disabled and uniting with the disability rights movement (Turnbull& Turnbull, 2000). 1974 brought the Family Educational Rights and Privacy Act of 1974 (a part of P.L. 99-457) commonly known as FERPA. FERPA was an amendment to the Elementary and Secondary Education Act (ESEA) providing that no federal funds would be made available to schools unless they adhered to strict record keeping procedures to maintain confidentiality.

In the 1980's during the Reagan administration, de-federalization began to take effect and local control in education again became more prevalent. In 1983 a report was issued "A Nation At-Risk" calling for curriculum reform by Federal government imposing its will on state and local government thereby increasing role of Federal government in education once again. During the late 1980's began a move away from focusing on curriculum reform to the structure of school and education in general. "A Nation Prepared," included the theory of "bottom up" structuring including total quality management. The theory was that schools should start at the bottom and go up with site-based management. It was again a reallocation of power with the Federal government still funding the process, but with fewer directives. The Goals 2000 Educating America Act advocated changing the system of education itself. In the systems reform process schools were to examine themselves with suggestions for reformation planning. Schools were required to report to the Federal government and implement the plan (Turnbull& Turnbull, 2000).

With the most current Federal mandates, IDEA 2004 and NCLB, the Federal government is again imposing standards and regulations for states and local boards to put into place. Some refer to IDEA 2004 and NCLB as un-funded mandates as there appear to be rules with severe penalties with little or no funding to implement with fidelity.

I feel that you are violating my parental rights and in doing so you are also infringing upon my child's right to her federally mandated free and appropriate public education.

CHAPTER 3
DISABILITY LAWS

The United States Congress is not allowed to create a nationalized school system; however, they do have the power to shape educational policies and implementation by offering monetary incentives to states contingent on their compliance with all federal mandates (Jacob & Hartshorne, 1991). These federal education laws are needed to address the history of discrimination in education perpetrated by state and local education agencies (Turnbull & Turnbull, 2000). As the federal legislation is enacted, it is put upon the individual states to interpret and implement the rules and regulations appropriately (Turnbull & Turnbull, 2002).

American Disability Act

The American Disability Act as discussed briefly in chapter 2 includes Section 504 which provides protections for those who are "otherwise qualified" when given reasonable accommodations. Basically, if a student with disabilities can be relatively successful with reasonable accommodations that will not substantially change the curriculum or cause extreme financial hardship to the district he or she may be eligible for a "504 Plan." The plan may be written by a team to define and ensure accommodations to help the child be successful in school. For example, if a child has a learning disability in written language and has difficulty taking notes quickly in class but is otherwise able to progress in the curriculum his or her 504 plan may include mandated accommodations (as developed with the team) like:

1) Student will be provided a copy of the teacher's notes or notes from a peer.

These accommodations may be applicable in multiple classes or settings if the student does not require more structured services through special education. If a child with disabilities has an Individual Education Program (IEP), the accommodations found in his or her IEP may eventually become a 504 plan upon graduation if the accommodation will help the child be successful in school or job setting after high school. The team will again make the determination regarding need.

What Constitutes Discrimination Under Section 504

To be protected by the ADA, a person must have a disability or have a relationship or association with an individual with a disability. An individual with a disability is defined by the ADA as a person who has a physical or mental impairment that substantially limits one or more major life activities, a person who has a history or record of such an impairment, or a person who is perceived by others as having such an impairment. The ADA does not specifically name all of the impairments that are covered. Discrimination under Section 504 can occur in many different forms and settings. Discrimination can be found in the exclusion of a person with disabilities; or inferior treatment/facilities; or even in the differential treatment that is not an appropriate response to the needs or capabilities of an individual with a disability. (U.S. Department of Justice)

Discrimination is defined in terms of specific actions that are either "not allowed to do"actions or "absolutely have to do"obligations, including:

- Denying a qualified individual with a disability the opportunity to participate in or benefit from an aid, benefit or service. This applies to all aspects of a school district's operations, including nonacademic and extracurricular activities.

- Affording a qualified individual with a disability an opportunity to participate in or benefit from an aid, benefit or service that is not equal to that afforded to others. OCR generally has frowned on separate treatment of students with disabilities, unless the treatment is justifiable as a reasonable modification for similar and comparable opportunity.

- Providing a qualified individual with a disability an aid, benefit or service that is not as effective as that provided to others. This requirement is called the "commensurate opportunity" standard. It is a regulation involving access to buildings and services.

- Providing different or separate aids, benefits or services to individuals with disabilities unless such action is necessary to provide them with aids, benefits or services that are as effective as those provided to others.

- Aiding or perpetuating discrimination against a qualified individual with a disability by providing significant assistance to an agency, organization or person that discriminates on the basis of disability in providing any aid, benefit or services.

- Denying a qualified individual with a disability the opportunity to participate as a member of planning or advisory boards.

- Otherwise limiting a qualified individual with a disability in the enjoyment of any right, privilege, advantage or opportunity enjoyed by others receiving an aid, benefit or service.

- Directly, or through contractual or other arrangements, using criteria or methods of administration that:

  o Have the effect of subjecting qualified individuals with disabilities to discrimination on the basis of disability.

  o Have the purpose of defeating or substantially impairing accomplishment of the objectives of the recipient's program with respect to individuals with disabilities.

  o Perpetuate the discrimination of another recipient if both recipients are subject to common administrative control or are agencies of the same state. (Office of Civil Rights, 34 CFR 104.4 (b)(1) i-vii.).

The Rules are Vague on 504 Placement Team Composition

According to Section 504 regulations, placement decisions must be made by "a group of persons," including those knowledgeable about the student, the meaning of the evaluation data, and the placement options. However, the regulations offer no other guidance further specifying who these "knowledgeable people" might be. Unlike the IEP team provisions of the IDEA, the Section 504 regulations do not identify individuals who must participate in the decision-making. The Section 504 regulations do not specify the number of individuals who must be included to constitute the team. IDEA does not govern the number of people required at IEP meetings either, but rather looks at whether a district includes a group of individuals who are knowledgeable about a student and his special needs. (U.S. Department of Education)

IDEA

IDEA provides legal entitlements to special education services and rights for students who (a) have a disability and (b) need special services because of the disability (Turnbull & Turnbull, 2000). Special education is defined as "specially designed instruction that meets the unusual needs of an exceptional student (Hallahan & Kaufman, 1994)." The current definition of learning disability, according to the state of Kansas, is K.A.R. 91-12-22(rr) is "a disorder in the ability to learn effectively with respect to one's own potential when presented with an appropriate regular instructional environment. The inability to learn effectively is manifested as a disorder in the ability to receive, organize, or express information relevant to school functioning, and is demonstrated by a significant discrepancy between aptitude and achievement in one or more of the following areas: pre-academic skills, oral expression, listening comprehension, written expression, basic reading skills, reading comprehension, mathematical calculation, and mathematical reasoning. This discrepancy shall not be primarily attributable to vision, hearing, or motor impairments; mental retardation; emotional disabilities; environmental, cultural, or economic disadvantage; or a history of an inconsistent educational program." States vary on legal definitions of learning disability. IDEA will be covered more in depth in chapter 4 of this handbook.

NCLB

The No Child Left Behind Act includes a performance based accountability process in which all children are tested in English and in math. If a school or district does not make adequate yearly progress (AYP), consequences will be implemented. If a school or district continues to fail to make AYP, Federal financing may be withheld. Parents are given the choice of removing their children to a school who makes AYP. If schools do not make AYP for 3 years children may choose to attend another public or private school. NCLB allows greater flexibility for utilizing Federal funding in terms of programs or professional development. The goal is for all children to read on grade level. Teachers must use evidence based instructional methods, which are research validated. (NCLB)

I feel that you are violating my parental rights and in doing so you are also infringing upon my child's right to her federally mandated free and appropriate public education.

Chapter 4
SPED Law IDEA 2004

Congress enacted the Individuals with Disabilities Education Act (IDEA). IDEA is an extremely detailed law, which requires school districts to document and justify all services provided to children eligible for special services. The law defines the obligation of States and local school districts to identify and serve all eligible students within their geographic boundaries (Lane, Connelly, Mead, Gooden, & Eckes, 2005).

The Executive branch is tasked with making sure that IDEA is implemented appropriately, and the Courts are expected to interpret the Act. Part A of IDEA includes the facts, purpose, and policy of special education. Part B of IDEA creates and defines the rights of students and the duties of educators. Part C describes and defines programs from birth to 3 for infants and toddlers. Part D of IDEA creates and defines national capacity for research and training programs.

IDEA is considered to be a civil rights statute by the EEOC as well as an educational statute. IDEA states that just as African American students had the right to go to school (Brown vs. Topeka BOE), so do people with disabilities. Under these auspices, all children will be assured the right to a Free and Appropriate Public Education (FAPE) (Turnbull & Turnbull, 2000). What is a Free and Appropriate Education for one child may not be for another. All decisions for each child must be made according to that child's needs NOT on program availability or group instruction. In order to meet the legal intent of a free and appropriate public education, the following elements of IDEA must be met:

Procedural Safeguards and Due Process

Procedural safeguards are intended to ensure fairness of educational decisions and placement along with accountability for both professionals and parents regarding these decisions. The safeguards referred to in IDEA 2004 include due process hearings, parental notice, parental consent, confidentiality of records and record keeping, independent evaluation, and access to records. The definition of "parent" for the purposes of special education is included. Chapter 5 of this handbook describes and details the safeguards more fully.

Appropriate Educational Placement and Related Services

IDEA is founded on the principle or ideal that what a child requires in order to be successful to the greatest extent appropriate with regular education peers may not necessarily be a "cookie cutter" service plan. IEP teams should closely evaluate, consider, and monitor services determined appropriate for each child. Schools are required to offer a continuum of services or alternative placements in order to best meet the special education needs of all children. These services or alternative placements may include, but are not limited to: supplementary aids and services; curricular adaptations and accommodations; medical, speech language, psychological, or social work supports; and resource rooms, special classes, and special schools.

A school must clearly demonstrate that a free and appropriate public education (FAPE) cannot occur within a regular education classroom before alternative settings may be considered. The courts interpret appropriate services in meeting FAPE, not as the "Cadillac" of services to meet all needs and wants fully, but to be "reasonably calculated to enable the child to receive educational benefits" (Lane et al, 2005).

Nondiscriminatory Evaluation

According to the IDEA, assessments must be provided and administered to the extent practicable in the "language and form most likely to yield accurate information on what the child knows and can do academically, functionally, and developmentally."

Once a child has been referred for a comprehensive evaluation, the team should review records and consider the best methods and assessments needed in order to determine if the child meets the requirements for placement in special education or receiving special education supports.   Few if any evaluation procedures alone provide accurate and reliable information or completely relevant results.

More than one examiner utilizing multiple techniques, methods, and assessments under standardized conditions when appropriate should conduct comprehensive multi-disciplinary evaluations. The team should consider all areas related to the child's potential needs including, health and physical, social and emotional development, academic performance, intelligence or ability, communication abilities, and motor abilities. No one person or assessment method should be able to determine eligibility for special education services.

Tests and assessment methods should be chosen based on the specific concerns regarding the child as well as considering the child and parents' language. A child's strengths and weaknesses should be considered in interpreting and accepting results (i.e., a verbally loaded test should not be used for a child with apparent speech language or receptive language concerns). A well-trained and ethical professional should choose appropriately for each individual child.

Individual Education Program

If a child is determined to meet the requirements for eligibility and placement in special education and the parents have given consent, the team should meet in order to design an Individual Education Program or IEP. An IEP is a document required by law, which defines a Free Appropriate Public Education for an individual child. The document defines the child's current levels of ability along with the services and placements required in order to best meet that child's special education needs. A child's unique strengths and needs dictate the goals and objectives outlined by the IEP. In chapter seven we will discuss the IEP more in-depth.

Least Restrictive Environment

IDEA requires that children with disabilities be educated in their Least Restrictive Environment. LRE requires that children be educated with their non-disabled peers to the greatest extent appropriate. Students should be provided with the LEAST amount of special education services and supports needed in order for them to progress with regular education peers in the regular education setting and curriculum. The tricky part is the term appropriate. Each child has unique and individual needs. What may be most appropriate for one child may not be appropriate for another. The team again must first consider individual needs in creating a child's IEP in the LRE.

Sometimes a child needs a MORE restrictive environment to meet his or her Least Restrictive Environment mandate. In other words, sometimes a child is unsuccessful with minimal supports and requires more supports or a different placement in order to be successful in his or her educational placement.

Frequently parents and educational teams disagree on what is a LRE. IDEA requires that a school is ultimately responsible for meeting a child's LRE for a free appropriate public education (FAPE). If a school and parent cannot come to agreement, and the school believes that the parent's requested placement or services is not what is most appropriate for the child, the school may initiate due process by law.

Parent Participation

IDEA maintains emphasis on parental involvement and participation. Parents generally understand and know their child better than anyone on the team. Schools are expected to encourage and enable active and meaningful involvement of parents. School districts may be required to provide reasonable accommodations to parents if necessary in order to have meaningful participation in their child's education. For instance, the school may be required to provide a sign language interpreter so that parents who are hearing impaired may participate in his or her child's IEP meeting. Schools would not be required to provide these accommodations for the parent for activities that would not be necessary like school concerts, plays, or ceremonies (Lane et al, 2005).

Barriers to Effective Involvement

The Individuals with Disabilities Education Act requires that parents be involved in and an integral part of the team in making educational decisions for a child with a disability; however, some parents, for a variety of reasons, do not attend the meetings. Single parents who work multiple jobs have a definitive amount of time to pick up their children, prepare meals, try to attend each child's activities outside of school, pay bills, do housework, and other daily responsibilities.

Some parents have experienced their own difficulties while attending school and, therefore, have to overcome their own haunting memories of education, educators, administration, and peer problems. Some parents have limited reading, writing, and communication skills, which if not treated delicately, may cause them to avoid the interaction with educators and "the system." Transportation and work schedules can be a deterrent for others. Parents of children with disabilities who have received numerous negative reports regarding their children, without positive input, may simply refuse to listen to another defamation of their child. IDEA also puts the responsibility on parents to be actively involved and pursue any opportunity to learn about and contribute to your child's education.

IDEA 2004

IDEA 2004 again calls for an overall paperwork reduction. Long has been the complaint by special educators that the majority of time spent involved paperwork not children (P.L. 108-446, sec. 609 (a)(1). Repeatedly the federal government has made allowances for this paperwork reduction; however, generally the reality is an increase rather than decrease in paperwork.

IDEA 2004 allows for the waiver of certain procedural safeguards particularly in the area of parent refusal to respond (i.e., to a request for meeting or permission).

IDEA also allows that a parent, State Education Agency (SEA), other state agency, or Local Education Agency (LEA) may request an initial evaluation for IDEA. Notice of Parental Transfer Rights revises provisions relating to transfer of parental rights at age of majority to allow a parent of a child with a disability to elect to receive required notices by email communication, if the public agency makes such option available. Notice of Parental Transfer Rights revises provisions relating to transfer of parental rights at age of majority to allow a parent of a child with a disability to elect to receive required notices by email communication, if the public agency makes such option available (LexisNexis, 2005).

IDEA 2004 calls for the same highly qualified teachers as regular education students are supposed to have according to the No Child Left Behind Act. Special education budgets as well as grants are being allocated for professional development of all staff in order to educate professionals on Response To Intervention, IDEA, Curriculum Based Measure, reasonable accommodation, and etc. As with NCLB, IDEA 2004 requires academic achievement accountability with reports including disaggregated data to include (but not limited to) the percentage of students with and without disabilities tested; the types of testing utilized; how many students with and without disabilities made Adequate Yearly Progress (AYP), the number of boys and girls with and without disabilities tested. IDEA 2004 allows Part B funds to be allocated to regular education (non-disabled children, early intervention services, high cost education and services, and administrative case management, including related technology.) LEAs may utilize 15% of IDEA funds to be used for professional development for staff towards delivery of scientifically based academic and behavioral interventions and providing educational and behavior evaluations, services, and supports, including scientifically-based literacy instruction.

Imputed Knowledge of Disability as defined in IDEA 2004 means that an LEA will not be expected to know that the child has a disability if the child's parent has not agreed to provide consent for an evaluation requested by the LEA. Furthermore, a child will have IDEA protections if he or she is not determined eligible for special education and related services who has violated a code of student conduct, if the LEA had knowledge that the child had a disability before the behavior that precipitated the disciplinary action occurred. Also supposes that an LEA has knowledge about a child's disability if: the parent has expressed concern in writing; the parent has requested an evaluation; or a teacher or other school personnel has expressed concern about a pattern of behavior to either the special education director, or to other administrative personnel (LexisNexis, 2005). So.....if a parent refuses to allow an evaluation requested by the school, the school is not expected to "know" if the child has a disability or protections under IDEA. However, the child may have IDEA protections called a "perceived disability" if a parent or teacher has asked for a comprehensive evaluation or expressed significant learning or behavioral concerns.

Parental Choice Involving Medications

The reauthorization specifically prohibits schools from requiring a child as a condition of attending school or receiving SPED evaluation or receiving services to obtain a prescription for medication covered by the Controlled Substances Act. This means that a school CANNOT require a child to be treated with medication for ADD in order to attend classes and/or activities.

I feel that you are violating my parental rights and in doing so you are also infringing upon my child's right to her federally mandated free and appropriate public education.

CHAPTER 5

YOU DECIDED WHAT
ABOUT MY CHILD WITHOUT ME?

Parental Safeguards

Parent, as defined by IDEA 2004, means, "a natural, adoptive, or foster parent of a child (unless a foster parent is prohibited by State law from serving as a parent); a guardian (but not the State if the child is a ward of the State); an individual acting in the place of a natural or adoptive parent (including a grandparent, stepparent, or other relative) with whom the child lives, or an individual who is legally responsible for the child's welfare; or except as used in sections 615(b)(2) and 639(a)(5), an individual assigned under either of those sections to be a surrogate parent."

Parents of children with special education needs have many federally protected rights. Generally these "rights" are provided in a packet to parents. Parents have told me, "I have enough of those things at home to wallpaper my bathroom!" Ideally, a principal or other administrative representative should present the rights to parents and explain in detail, unfortunately this does not always happen. Instead, a parent may be handed the packet and asked, without an explanation of the information, "Do you have any questions?"

These rights are an important part of the federally protected mandate and it is important to read the packet fully and to ask any questions you may have about these rights.

Parents have the right to receive a written notice within a reasonable amount of time before the school district PROPOSES or REFUSES to initiate or change the identification, evaluation or educational placement of your child or the provision of a free appropriate public education to your child.

A *reasonable amount of time* is certainly subjective and may be outlined by the state or individual district depending on specific guidelines. Generally ten days notice is considered a reasonable amount of time. Receiving a call at work in the afternoon telling a parent that an IEP meeting is scheduled before school the following morning would *not* be considered a reasonable amount of time.

The intent of IDEA is to schedule meetings around a parent's schedule, not around the teacher's plan periods or coaching responsibilities. However, NEA contracts being what they are, teachers may be very reluctant to meet before or after their scheduled workday.

"I'm at work. No Bill cannot make it then either. What about Wednesday at 4:30, we're both off then. I realize that, but we both have to work. We've had to reschedule this four times already. No, we both need to be there. Is there any way they will stay later? Could you ask? Well okay, I guess we'll try to get the time off again. But I've only been at this job for 3 months and I've had to take off twice already to meet with you. I'm not sure if my boss will allow it."

** One side of a phone call from a parent to an LD Teacher.

If a parent is concerned with meetings not being set appropriate to his or her schedule, or that a reasonable amount of notice is not being provided, the principal or special education director should be contacted.

The notice of meeting shall include:

- a description of the action proposed or refused by the school district;

- an explanation of why the action is proposed or refused;

- a description a of each evaluation procedure, test, record, or report used as a basis for the action proposed or refused;

- a description of any other factors relevant to the school district's decision;

- a statement that you have protection under the procedural safeguards set forth in the federal law, and the means by which you may obtain a copy of a description of those procedural safeguards; and

- sources for you to contact to obtain assistance in understanding your rights.

A description of the action proposed or refused by a school may be: changing the amount of time a child receives special education support; changing where he or she receives support (i.e., in the regular classroom with peers, in the special education classroom, in the regular classroom with a paraprofessional's support, and etc.); adding services; exiting a program; or other. An explanation of why the action is proposed or refused is required in order to justify the changes the team is proposing. The changes need to be made in order to best meet a child's LRE and providing a FAPE, not because it best fits the school's schedule.

An explanation of why the action is proposed or refused is required to demonstrate that the team took into account various options for service and decided on the program which would best meet the child's individual needs. A description of each evaluation procedure, test, record, or report used as a basis for the team's decision is required for accountability purposes and to further provide evidence that the decision is student-focused. Phone numbers or websites of support resources are provided with the parent rights, for parents to obtain further clarification of any questions he or she may have. These resources may also be used in making a complaint if parent rights are being violated.

A copy of the procedural safeguards must be given to the parent, at a minimum:

- upon initial referral for evaluation

- upon each notification of an individualized education program meeting;

- upon reevaluation of the child;

and

- upon filing for a due process hearing.

This notice must be in writing at a level understandable to the general public and provided in the parents' native language or other principle method of communication unless it is clearly not feasible to do so. If the parent's method of communication is not a written language, he or she has the right to be notified orally or by other means. The school district must take steps to ensure that the parent understands the information provided in the notice.

Clearly, the federal government is trying to provide the information in the most "readable" or understandable terms possible. Unfortunately, the language utilized can still be confusing even to educators. When in doubt ask questions of the team or utilize the numbers provided in the packet. The State Department of Education is also good resource for any special education related question.

Consent

Consent means:

- That a parent has been fully informed in his or her native language or other mode of communication of all information relevant to the activity for which consent is sought;

- that a parent understands and agree in writing to the activity for which his or her consent is sought;

- there is a description of the activity and lists of records (if any) which will be released and to whom; and

- that written consent is voluntary and may be revoked at any time.

The team must make every reasonable attempt to explain fully to what a parent is giving his or her "okay." A parent should not give lawful and binding consent without complete understanding. Frequently a parent is expected to give consent to a placement or service change the same day he or she is provided the information regarding his or her child's disability. A parent should explain that they need time to digest the information and talk to (spouse, support, advocate, or other) before making any binding decision. To be an effective child advocate, a parent must make every effort to be fully informed regarding any special education decision.

Written consent must be obtained before a school district conducts an initial evaluation or reevaluation for a student and before the district makes an initial placement into a special education program. Consent for an evaluation will not be construed as consent for initial placement. Consent may be withheld, withdrawn, or revoked at any time. If consent is revoked, the revocation is not retroactive which means that your revocation of consent does not negate an action that has occurred after your consent was given but before consent was revoked. If consent is refused, the school district must take appropriate action which may include the initiation of a due process hearing to determine if the child may still be evaluated, reevaluated, or initially placed in a special education program without consent. If the hearing officer upholds the school district, an initial evaluation, reevaluation, or initial placement in a special education program may be provided subject to your right to appeal the hear officer's decision.

Before a school district may begin evaluating a child, written permission must be obtained from a parent. Providing consent for an initial evaluation does not automatically give them permission to place your child in special education. A parent may refuse to give permission, or may change their mind a take back their permission. If a parent changes his or her mind and revokes or takes back their permission, any evaluation data or results already obtained will not be destroyed. The revocation is not, therefore, retroactive. One of the reasons is if a parent again changes his or her mind and wants the school to proceed, the child is not put back through the same testing. Some tests may only ethically be given once a year.

A school district may decide that they believe testing or placement is needed enough to start due process hearings to see if a parent's refusal can be overturned. If the hearing officer agrees with the school, the child may be tested or placed at least until an appeal is filed. Parent advocacy groups, Internet supports, and State department officials are all good resources for information regarding the process.

Parental consent is not required before reviewing existing data as part of an evaluation or reevaluation or administering a test or other evaluation that is given to all children unless, before giving the test or evaluation, consent is required of parents of all children. If a school district has attempted to obtain your consent for a reevaluation with no response, the district may conduct the evaluation without consent, provided that the school district can demonstrate that it had taken reasonable efforts to obtain consent and failed to gain a response to the requests. A school district may not used a parent's refusal to consent to one service or activity to deny the parent or child any other service, benefit, or activity of the school district, except as required by state statute or guideline.

Usually the school does not need parental permission to look at the information they already have. If a school makes a good faith effort to obtain parental permission without a response, the evaluation may occur. The school must be able to demonstrate that reasonable efforts were made to gain consent. An example might be documentation that the school tried by phone, by mail, and in person to contact the parent (this is only an example not a mandate). The school cannot punish the child by not allowing him or her to participate in other school related activities as retribution for a parent's refusal to allow an evaluation unless it is required by the state.

Records

1. Parents or guardians have the right to inspect and review all education records with respect to the identification, evaluation, and educational placement of their child and the provision of a free appropriate public education.

2. The request to review records must:

   a. occur without unnecessary delay

   b. prior to any meeting regarding an individualized education program or hearing relating to the identification, evaluation, or placement of a child;

   and

   c. no later than 45 days from request.

3. The school district must respond to reasonable requests for explanations and interpretations of the information in the records.

4. Upon request, a list of the types and location of education records collected, maintained or used by the school district will be provided.

5. The school district will provide copies of the records if failure to obtain copies would keep a parent or guardian from reviewing or inspecting the records. The school district may not charge a fee to search for or to retrieve records.

6. A representative of your choice may inspect and review the records.

7. Consent may be given or withheld to disclosing records.

8. The school district must maintain a log of persons obtaining access to a child's records which includes the name of the party, date access was given, and the purpose for which the party is authorized to use the records.

9. If the record contains information about another child, only information relating to your child may be inspected and reviewed.

10. The school district may presume that a parent or guardian has the authority to look at records relating to his or her child unless the school district has been provided information that denies the parent or guardian authority under state law (guardianship, divorce).

11. A parent may request that the school district amend the information in the record if it is believed that the information is inaccurate or misleading or violates the privacy or other rights of the child. If the school district agrees to amend the education record, the record must be amended within a reasonable period of time.

12. A hearing may be requested if the school district refuses to amend the record. A hearing must be provided if requested. If, as a result of the hearing, the school district decides that the information is:

    a. inaccurate, misleading or a violation of privacy, the district must amend the record and inform you in writing of the amendment.

    b. not inaccurate, misleading or a violation of privacy, the district must inform the parents of the right to place in the records a statement setting forth the reasons for a parent disagreeing with the school district's decision. This statement must be maintained with the contested portion of the record as part of the education record as long as the record is maintained by the school district and included with any request for disclosure.

13. Request the destruction of information in a child's special education records (or be informed of the school district's proposed destruction of information in a child's special education records) when the information is no longer needed to provide education programs.

Evaluation

Evaluation means the procedures used to determine whether a child has a disability and the nature and extent of the special education and related services needed. An evaluation should be multi-modal and non-discriminatory. No one tool may be used in determining whether a child qualifies for special education services. A special education evaluation includes information provided by the parents. With the implementation of RTI, evaluations may become less testing and more figuring out what works best for individual children's learning styles utilizing scientifically based interventions. One good reason to maintain some "formal" test measures is the ability to compare a child's progress in comparison to a larger group of students (i.e., state or nationally normed tests). Most informal tests will compare a child to him or herself (progress) or compare to the class, school, or district only.

Independent Educational Evaluations

An independent educational evaluation is an evaluation conducted by a qualified examiner who is not employed by the public school responsible for the child's education. A parent has the right to request an independent educational evaluation at public expense if he or she disagrees with the educational evaluation provided by the school district. Public expense means that the public school either pays for the full cost of the evaluation or insures that the evaluation is otherwise provided at no cost to the parent. The school district is obligated to provide the information upon request as to how and where to obtain an independent evaluation and the district's criteria applicable for independent educational evaluations. If an independent educational evaluation is at public expense, the criteria under which the evaluation is obtained, including the location of the evaluation and the qualifications of the examiner, must be the same as the criteria that the school district uses when it initiates an evaluation (to the extent that those criteria are consistent with the parent's right to an independent educational evaluation). Except for the district's criteria, the district may not impose conditions or timelines related to obtaining an independent educational evaluation. If a parent requests an independent educational evaluation, the school may ask for the reason for objecting to the district's evaluation. However, an explanation may not be required and the district may not unreasonably delay either providing the independent educational evaluation or initiating a due process hearing to demonstrate the appropriateness of the district's evaluation.

The school may initiate a due process hearing to show that its evaluation is appropriate. If a hearing officer requests an independent educational evaluation as part of the hearing, the cost of the evaluation must be at public expense. If the final decision in the hearing is that the school district's evaluation is appropriate, parents still have a right to an independent educational evaluation but not at public expense. If a parent obtains an independent educational evaluation at their own expense, the school district must consider the results of the independent educational evaluation in any decision it makes about their child's educational program.

Results of an independent educational evaluation may be presented at a due process hearing.

Parent Participation

Parents have the right to participate in all decision-making meetings involving their child. Parents should be included from the time a team first meets with concerns until the time when placement decisions are being made. Parents should be encouraged to ask questions, make suggestions, offer insights, and any other contribution expected of a valued team member.

Unilateral Placement by Parents of Children into Nonpublic Schools

According to IDEA 2004, school districts are required to provide funding for parentally – placed private school children with disabilities under certain conditions. LEAs are directed to provide direct services to the extent it is practicable. These services must be secular, neutral, and nonideological. If the State or LEA places a child in private school to receive required special education services, it will be at no cost to the parents. If parents place their child in private school due to suspicion that their child is not receiving a FAPE and a hearing officer or court orders in the parent's favor, the parents should be reimbursed.

The text in bold was taken directly from the parent rights form I was handed at my own son's IEP meeting. (Parental Rights in Special Education, Revised September 1999, Nebraska Department Education. All states may have slightly different language. Most will probably be revised following the implementation of IDEA 2004).

I feel that you are violating my parental rights and in doing so you are also infringing upon my child's right to her federally mandated free and appropriate public education.

Chapter 6
My Child Did *What* to *Whom*?
Alternative Placements

IDEA 2004 authorizes schools to consider any unique circumstances on a case-by-case basis when determining whether to order a change in placement for a child with a disability who violates 'a code of student conduct.' This may be troubling as a parent considering the vagueness of the term 'violates a code of student conduct.' Yet to be seen is the State and LEA interpretation of the language. Considering the verbiage, a child could conceivably have a school ordered change in placement if he or she talked during class (extreme example, but thought provoking). In this day and age of student on student violence, the intent of the change is probably in allowing school officials and teams more power in enforcing school rules; however, the broadness of the language can be somewhat disturbing. Schools are allowed to change the placement to an appropriate interim educational setting, another setting, or suspension for up to 10 consecutive school days for children with disabilities who violate a student code of conduct.

Shelley Smith

Manifestation Determination Hearings and Placement

Schools are required to review all relevant information by the LEA, parent, and IEP team within 10 school days of such a disciplinary decision as a change of placement to determine if the child's behavior was a manifestation of his or her disability based on whether the conduct was: a) caused by, or had a direct and substantial relationship to the child's disability; or b) was the direct result of the LEA's failure to implement the IEP appropriately (IDEA 2004-P.L. 108-446). If the child's IEP has clear goals, objectives, or a behavior plan to effectively address the behavior and the school fails to implement said plan, this should not be held against the student. A manifestation of a disability means that the behavior was caused by the child's disability or he or she could not control the behavior due to the disability. Another manifestation of a disability might be the child's inability to understand the consequences of his or her actions due to the disability.

A Manifestation Hearing was scheduled due to John's actions and concurrent consequences. The LEA wanted to expel John for holding box cutters up to a teacher and threatening to cut her throat during art class. As part of the review process, all parties were interviewed including John. When asked why John said what he did, he responded with a blank stare and repeatedly said, "I don't know." When asked if John meant to kill or hurt the teacher, John emphatically replied, "No! Never! That would be bad."

When asked what the difference was between what he said and what the interviewer said, John again responded with a blank stare and, "I don't know." Upon review of the records it was revealed to the team that John had a Verbal IQ well under 70, the general cutoff score to consider a Mental Retardation label. After further questioning in which John demonstrated to the team that he did not understand his actions or the consequences, the team agreed the behavior WAS a manifestation of his disability and therefore John would not be expelled or held out of school suspended for longer than 10 days. The IEP and Behavior Plan were reviewed and appropriate modifications were made.

If the conduct is found to be a manifestation of a disability, or out of the child's control due to his or her disability, the IEP team is required to: conduct a functional behavioral assessment and implement an appropriate behavioral intervention plan with positive behavioral supports if the LEA has not already done so. If a behavioral intervention plan has already been developed, the team is required to review and modify the plan, if appropriate, to address the behavior of concern; and (except in cases involving weapons, drugs, or infliction of serious bodily injury) return the child to the placement from which he or she was removed, unless the parent and LEA agree to a change of placement as part of the modification of the behavioral intervention plan (IDEA 2004-P.L. 108-446). In other words, the child will continue to receive the same services in the same placement as prior to the offense with some modification possible, unless the team and parent agree to a change.

A functional behavioral assessment is an assessment of why a behavior occurs; what the behavior is; what may or may not reinforce the behavior; what can extinguish (eliminate) the unacceptable behavior; and who should do, change, or monitor in regards to the behavior. This is a precursor to creating a Behavior Intervention Plan. The theory behind functional behavior analysis is that every behavior supposedly has a purpose. The purpose can be one of two choices, either being rewarded or avoidance. If the purpose of the behavior can be appropriately identified, a systematic intervention in the form of a behavior intervention plan may be helpful in reshaping more appropriate or socially acceptable behaviors.

Schools may, upon determining that the violation in question was NOT a manifestation of the child's disability, apply the same disciplinary procedures as would apply for a child without disability. If it is NOT a manifestation of a disability, the child should and could have controlled the behavior and understood the consequences thereof. However, FAPE requirements must continue to be met. The child must still receive special education support to allow him or her to progress in the curriculum, but the services may be provided in an alternative educational setting and may be greatly reduced in the amount of time served as determined by the team. This is considered part of the 10-day rule in that the disciplinary action may apply beyond the 10-day period.

Weapons or Drugs

The weapons serious injury clause authorizes a school, in cases involving weapons or drugs, or when a child has committed serious bodily injury, to remove the child from the regular classroom setting for up to 45 school days, regardless of whether the child's behavior was a manifestation of disability. The clause requires that such children continue to receive educational services and the appropriate functional behavioral assessments, behavioral intervention services, and modifications to continue to provide a FAPE (IDEA 2004-P.L. 108-446).

Disciplinary Hearings

IEP teams are directed to determine the child's alternative educations setting. Examples of alternative settings could be (but are not limited to) the public library, a local justice building, an alternative school or other. IDEA 2004 sets forth circumstances in which a parent or LEA may request a hearing regarding disciplinary decisions or proposed disciplinary actions. A parent may disagree with the LEA decisions regarding disciplinary actions, placements, or manifestation determination. Or, LEAs may believe that maintaining the child's current placement is substantially likely to result in injury to the child or others. During a parent's appeal, a child must remain in the interim alternative educational setting chosen by the IEP team pending the hearing officer's decision or until the time period for the disciplinary action expires, whichever occurs first, unless the parent and public agency agree otherwise. The hearing must occur within 20 days of the hearing request. Parents and teams must be given a definitive result in a determination within 10 days after the hearing (IDEA 2004-P.L. 108-446).

I feel that you are violating my parental rights and in doing so you are also infringing upon my child's right to her federally mandated free and appropriate public education.

Chapter 7
IEP

An Individualized Education Program

An individualized education program is a binding contract which that is a written education plan for a school-aged child with disabilities developed by a team of professionals (teachers, therapists, etc.) and the child's parents. IEP's are based on a multidisciplinary evaluation of the child, describes how the child is presently doing, what the child's learning needs are, and what services the child will need. They are reviewed and updated at least yearly. IEP's are required under Public Law 94-142, the Individuals with Disabilities Education Act (IDEA). For children ages birth through 2 years, an IFSP is written. (U.S. Department of Education)

Parents should always be provided with a copy of the IEP and a copy should be accessible to every service provider responsible to implementation. Each and every teacher or service provider must be informed of his or her specific responsibilities in implementing the IEP.

IDEA 2004 includes the required components for an IEP. Statements of current levels of performance and functional performance are required. These may include recent test scores, grades, classroom participation, CBM progress or other applicable information. IDEA 2004 requires a statement of measurable annual goals, and eliminates requirements for benchmarks and short-term objectives in the IEPs. IEP's are required to contain descriptions of: how the child's progress toward meeting the annual goals will be measured; and when periodic progress reports will be provided. LEA's are required to provide parents with progress updates with specific, meaningful, and understandable information on the progress children are making. I love language like this, as one person's "meaningful and specific" may be another person's, "Huh?"

IDEA 2004 requires an explanation of the extent, if any, that the child will not participate in class and extracurricular and non-academic activities with non disabled children. An explanation of supplementary aids and services and classroom modifications is required. The IEP must also contain listed supports for school personnel, level of participation in district and state assessments, transition goals and services, extended school year when appropriate, how progress will be measured and the method for reporting to parents.

IDEA 2004 requires IEP teams to provide positive behavioral interventions and supports for children with disabilities whose behavior impedes their learning or the learning of others.

Accommodations and Alternate Assessment

Requirements for accommodations and alternate assessments have been somewhat revised with the new authorization as well. IDEA 2004 provides for testing of some children that includes certain necessary accommodations, an alternate assessment, or an alternate assessment based upon alternative standards for those children with significant cognitive disabilities. The key is the term "significant cognitive need" and only a very minute percentage of the population qualifies accordingly.

The IEP requires a statement of exactly what appropriate accommodations are to be made for a child on State or district wide assessments. These accommodations cannot be specific only for State or district wide assessments. The child must need the same accommodations in other forms of work or assessment for it to be considered a valid need of statement on the IEP. The IEP team is required, if it determines that a child shall take an alternate assessment, to state why the child cannot participate in the regular assessment and why the particular alternate assessment selected is appropriate for that child. These requirements are an attempt to align IDEA more fully with the assessment standards of NCLB.

Transition Services

In the previous authorization transition services plans were to be addressed no later than the year before a child's 14th birthday. Now IDEA requires that IEPs beginning not later than the first IEP to be in effect when the child is 16, and updated annually thereafter, to contain: appropriate measurable postsecondary goals based upon age appropriate assessments related to training, education, employment, and where appropriate independent living skills; and the transition services the child needs to reach those goals. These needs may be as little as a statement of, "Johnny's transition goals will be met through the regular education curriculum," to a more formal transition team functional placement strategy depending on the individual student's needs.

Students who are "exiting" special education due to graduation or "aging out" must be provided a summary of academic and functional performance with recommendations to assist them in meeting transition goals.

IEP-Team meetings

IEP teams should consist of parents, student (when appropriate) regular classroom teachers, special education teacher/service provider, district representative, others with knowledge or expertise, individual capable of interpreting the instructional implications of the evaluation (usually a school psychologist or special education teacher), other agency representatives like transition services, and a representative from private school if relevant.

IDEA 2004 allows members of the IEP team to be excused from an IEP meeting if the parent consents and the curricular area will not be discussed. If curricular area will be discussed, the member can still be excused with parent permission and the excused member provides written input for the team. IDEA 2004 allows parents and LEA's to agree to participate in IEP team and placement meetings via means such as videoconferences and conference calls.

I feel that you are violating my parental rights and in doing so you are also infringing upon my child's right to her federally mandated free and appropriate public education.

Chapter 8
How Do they Decide?

Over the past 25 years, the percentage of students placed in programs for Learning Disabilities has increased to the point that 50% of all students in special education are labeled learning disabled (Fuchs, Fuchs, & Speece, 2002). The debate over the discrepancy model for placement in learning disability programs has been ongoing. Recently, a model utilizing a student's response to intervention as a replacement model has been studied. This approach to identification utilizing an intervention responsiveness approach (Fuchs, 2003), attempts to examine levels of student performance, gauge the effects of individual student adaptation to regular education interventions and accommodations, and finally verify the effectiveness of special education programming prior to placement (Fuchs, et al, 2002).

Regular Education Intervention

General education intervention, previously termed "pre-assessment," is based in the problem-solving model. According to KAR 91-40-7(c)(2), the team is flexible and should be determine by the area(s) of concern including age and needs of the child. In addition to the parents of the child, the team may consist of: building principal, referring teacher, regular education teachers, special education teachers, counselor, transition coordinator, related services personnel, school nurse, Title I or Section 504 coordinator, or others as deemed appropriate by the team.

The team bases their interventions on a child's strengths and concerns. The team attempts to remediate the child's concerns through regular education interventions. When a child demonstrates a need for supports or is struggling behind his or her peers, the team meets to discuss potential accommodations and supports needed in order to best meet the child's needs. A child may not be referred for a comprehensive evaluation until such time that a team has documented the exhaustion of regular education intervention supports, and they suspect that the child has a disability or the parent requests the evaluation and the school agrees that the evaluation is appropriate.

Comprehensive Evaluation

Non-discriminatory evaluation is required in order to determine the potential special education needs of a student. The evaluation should measure all aspects of the child's functioning. IDEA requires a multidisciplinary, multifaceted, unbiased comprehensive evaluation (Turnbull & Turnbull, 2000). Guidelines for assessment include, utilizing culturally sensitive, valid and reliable methods, by a highly trained professional trained to interpret scores in light of the child's cultural background, primary language, and any exceptional conditions. Tests are powerful instruments, but effectiveness depends on the skill and knowledge of the person interpreting the results (Sattler, 1992). School psychologists play an important role in this process as they have been traditionally considered the "gatekeepers" to special education, a researcher for disability, and a committed professional to be proactive versus reactive in the search for appropriate supports (Thomas & Grimes, 1995). A comprehensive evaluation must include, but is not limited to, a review of records and general education interventions, formal and informal evaluation, appropriate assessment batteries, interviews with parents, students, and teachers, observations, and other instruments as the team deems appropriate.

Identification and Placement

Federal Regulation: Sec 300.540 mandates that the determination of whether or not a child suspected of having a specific learning disability must be made by the child's parents and a team of qualified professionals which must include the child's regular education teacher, at least one person qualified to conduct individual diagnostic examinations and interpret such information such as a school psychologist, speech language pathologist, or remedial reading teacher. Prior to the most recent reauthorization, the team was required to determine if a suspected student demonstrated a severe discrepancy between ability and achievement. Meaning the child's achievement in math, reading, writing, or language was significantly different than the child's measure of ability (commonly referred to as IQ score).

The reauthorization of IDEA, removed the requirement to show a discrepancy between ability and achievement using an IQ test. This does not indicate that ability testing will be banned, but there will be a strong possibility that psychologists will forgo this vital piece of the comprehensive evaluation as it is very time consuming and many may not have adequate training in interpretation, thus not embracing the crucial information it can contribute to the evaluation process.

Response To Intervention Models

Concern regarding the process of identification of students with learning disabilities continues as learning disabilities are considered a "soft" disability, where no medical or physical marker is readily identifiable (Fuchs et al., 2002). Critics of traditional ability testing question the appropriateness of using child-based characteristics for treatment matching rather than classroom accommodation and varied instructional interventions.

Some special education leadership staff view conducting ability tests on all students considered for special education to be problematic and recommend only conducting intelligence tests when the team deems it to be appropriate and essential for the referred student. Public awareness of the scientific controversy has grown. The cost of special education compared to regular education is one of the defining issues. Further is the phenomenon of minority overrepresentation in special education (Fuchs et al., 2003). Redefining learning disabilities as inadequate response to instruction is the basis for the Response to

Intervention models (Vaughn & Fuchs, 2003). Response to Instruction models focus on the context of learning and instruction as a potential reason for the child's difficulties rather than automatically considering the problems to be a "child's deficit" (Fuchs, et al., 2003).

Treatment Validity Model

The treatment-validity model is considered to be the most developed conceptualization of how this RTI model may be applied to the LD identification process (Speece et al., 2003). In the Treatment Validity approach, three key questions must be answered: Is learning in the current instructional environment appropriate and effective? If not, can the regular classroom teaching be modified to induce appropriate learning? If not, does the child demonstrate more appropriate learning with special education supports (Elliott & Fuchs, 1997).

In this model, curriculum based measures (CBM) are utilized in regular education classrooms for all children (Speece et al., 2003). Curriculum based measure is a set of methods for tracking achievement and growth in basic academic skills. CBM allows for sampling directly from the curriculum to create an overall indicator of curriculum proficiency (Elliott & Fuchs, 1997). The level and rate (slope) of performance are monitored closely. Those children who have a discrepant level and slope (dual discrepancy) are targeted for intensive regular education instruction intervention. This method would be considered successful if the child improves in level and slope (treatment valid).

For the child that does not appear to respond, a placement in a trial special education program may be next to determine the level of responsiveness (Speece, et al., 2003). A controversial fourth phase required the added value of special education be demonstrated in order for the child to remain in special education. If the child does not make academic gains during this controversial fourth phase, the child is no longer eligible for services. Arguments against this fourth phase included the chance of false positives and those children who fail to respond may actually be the ones who most need the supports. A revised treatment model allowed for continued assessments and supports (Fuchs, Fuchs, & Speece, 2002).

Problem-Solving Model (PSM)

The PSM approach was developed as an alternative method to determining eligibility for special education. The model is based on a sequence of problem-solving steps for supporting and identifying potential student needs. The first step includes identifying specific strengths and weaknesses in performance to best make educational decisions for the child. Next, the team generates instructional accommodations to match the student's needs. The interventions must be implemented with fidelity to assure appropriate decision-making.

Staff collects data regarding the efficacy of the instructional model utilizing sensitive measures like CBM. The team utilizes these data at six to eight week intervals. The team then repeats the cycle as often as necessary to monitor and maintain growth. Stage one of the model addresses classroom interventions. Stage two involves problem-solving team interventions. If reasonable accommodations and interventions appear to be inadequate, the child is referred for special education evaluation. Using the PSM model, the team draws on the information from health records, review of the student's responses to interventions, consider formal measures of adaptive behavior, ecologically-based observation in learning environments, and direct student interaction which may or may not include formal standardized testing (Martson et al., 2003).

Ability Testing in Comprehensive Evaluation

"School psychology was born in the prison of a test-and this was certainly an intelligence test (Canter, 1997)." Numerous attacks have been made on the use of intelligence tests. Many center on cultural and socioeconomic bias. However, the critics fail to take into account the many valid uses of ability testing. Tests provide for accountability, normative reference, measurement of change, and evaluation opportunities for program effectiveness (Sattler, 1992).

Prior to the reauthorization of IDEA, (prior to July 5, 2005) a comprehensive evaluation included ability testing in that a child's own ability was compared to a child's own achievement. If the child demonstrates an average ability score and has one or more significantly discrepant areas of achievement, the child may have a learning disability. If the child struggles academically, but his level of achievement is commensurate with his ability, he or she may be a slow learner and in need of regular education accommodations rather than special education supports. Because a child struggles academically, it does not necessarily infer that child has a disability.

Placing children in special education who do not meet the placement criteria not only violates their civil rights, but also takes responsibility from regular education to create sound and effective teaching methods to support these children. Advantages to including ability testing in a comprehensive evaluation are: obtaining a more full and accurate understanding of the child and his her abilities, learning styles, and needs. The ability to analyze the profile results for a unique ability pattern which may be utilized in planning programs to utilize those strengths (Sattler, 1992). Disadvantages include the extensive amount of time involved in administering and interpreting the test scores. Administrators may believe their school psychologist's time could be spent in a more proactive way.

Curriculum Based Measurement

Advantages of incorporating CBM in the identification process include the ease of implementation. Teachers can literally monitor every student, every day, in a few minutes. Charting progress can be quickly done on a daily, weekly or even monthly basis. A teacher can quickly see if a child is advancing, reaching a plateau or declining and can adjust the teaching style accordingly. CBM is a direct reflection of how a child is performing within his or her own curriculum compared to his or her own peers. Disadvantages include the time and cost of norming a school or district. By the time the norming process is statistically complete, the results are virtually invalid as the child will be compared to the previous year's students and curriculum rather than their own. Furthermore, utilizing CBM only narrows the view. A child should still be compared, not only to local or class norms, but state and national as well for a comprehensive overview (Shinn, 1989).

Problems Associated With the Discrepancy Model Currently in Use

Studies have been done in which it has been ascertained that students in LD programs do not meet the discrepancy formula criteria as learning disabled. A study asked members of the editorial boards of scholarly journals if IQ-achievement should be used in defining reading disabilities, seventy percent agreed that it should play no role in the identification process (Fuchs et al., 2003). Although the argument could be and is made that the discrepancy model must be flawed, so too could the argument be made that if teams were to truly follow the law and guidelines regarding qualification criteria there would not be overrepresentation of minority, low socio-economic students, or the ever increasing rise in special education placement. Such inconsistencies of practice have led to a widespread view that the "LD designation is arbitrary" (Fuchs, et al., 2003).

Implications of Dropping the Discrepancy Model in Favor of the RTI Approach

The key term of contention in the definition of specific learning disability may then be "with respect to one's own potential." Attempts have been made to design the perfect assessment to measure ability. The assessment process should never depend on one score, or one battery of tests (Sattler, 1992). Tests for measures of ability do not purport to provide an exact score regarding a child's intelligence, but rather an indication of the child's ability to perform within a traditional school system. The "score" may be used as a reflection of the child's academic potential. Without this ipsative information, "with respect to one's own potential" will have to be redefined as "with respect to one's peers' potential."

Certainly eliminating the requirement for ability testing will leave many gifted, learning disabled students unnoticed, as well as eliminate the ability to gain insightful information from the results of these measures. However, changing the identification to include the response to intervention model by incorporating CBM monitoring may increase the team's ability to identify and support struggling students more quickly and effectively. Obliterating the need for a normative view of the child may well be throwing the proverbial baby out with the bath water.

Potential Implications of the RTI Model for the NCLB Safe Harbor Provision for Students With Disabilities

In removing the IQ-achievement discrepancy, the demonstration of a disability is no longer required. As low achievers are diagnosed with dual discrepancy and continue to demonstrate a lack of adequate progress, teams may feel pressured by the No Child Left Behind mandates that all must demonstrate adequate yearly progress, to place children in special education thus increasing false positives. The Safe Harbor provision within NCLB allows that schools who do not meet adequate yearly progress due to special education disaggregate scores may not be penalized if they can show a 10% reduction in those who do not make AYP the following year.

As it is already clear in literature and in practice that many teams do not implement regular education interventions with fidelity and disregard placement criteria by placing students who do not demonstrate a disability, but are low achievers, obliterating the need for a discrepancy score and encouraging teams to place struggling students will certainly not reduce the number and cost of special education, but instead open the flood gates to greater numbers of placements.

I feel that you are violating my parental rights and in doing so you are also infringing upon my child's right to her federally mandated free and appropriate public education.

CHAPTER 9
NOW WHAT?!

Talk to parents of children who have special needs. Form networks and alliances with organizations in the community or through the web. Be knowledgeable about your rights. Ask for and keep copies of all notes from meetings. Keep copies of all IEPs, comprehensive evaluation reports, notes, progress reports and other forms of communication in binder to take with you to meetings and to refer back to quickly and easily. What if they will not provide them you ask? Remember "the quote." *I feel that you are violating my parental rights and in doing so you are also infringing upon my child's right to her federally mandated free and appropriate public education.* Ask questions or call back for clarification on anything you do not understand. Ask a school psychologist or other child advocate if you believe that your child's rights are being infringed upon. Never be okay with NOT understanding. When in doubt, call state department or representative.

Remember the "Seven Deadliest Sins"

The State department will take complaints regarding the following very seriously:

1. Procedural violations

    - Failure to provide written notice with

    - A full explanation of procedural safeguards

    - Description of the proposed action

    - Options considered and why rejected

    - Description of each evaluation or test

    - Failure to obtain consent prior

        o   Initial evaluation

        o   Initial placement

        o   Release of records

    - Independent Evaluation

        o   Parents have the right to an IEE if they disagree with the district's evaluation

        o   Schools must either agree to an IEE and pay for or go to a hearing

        o   School districts must consider results of an IEE no matter who pays for it

- Incomplete/insufficient IEP

  o No goals for identified needs

  o Poor annual goals

  o Failure to complete IEP because parent and district cannot agree

  o Failure to plan in advance for transition and graduation

  o Improper Evaluations

- Delay in reevaluations

- Failure to evaluate all students suspected of having a disability

- Improper change of placement

  o Failure to provide notice

  o Failure to allow reasonable time for parents to challenge placement decisions

2. Denial of Services Based on Cost

   - Cost is not a defense for the failure to provide a FAPE

   - Cost may be a consideration when choosing between two appropriate placements

3. Program Rigidity

   - The district's programs must be flexible enough to meet the needs of all children regardless of need.

- District must meet the student's needs whether or not it currently offers a particular program

4. Giving in to Parents Even When it Violates a Child's Right to a FAPE

   - The right to a FAPE is the child's

   - Parents participate in the process but it is ultimately the school districts responsibility to ensure a FAPE

5. Principle vs. Reason

   - Consider the intent of the law as well as the letter of the law

6. Burden of Proof

   - Usually the burden of proof is on the school district

   - It is not enough to show the inappropriateness of the parent's proposal, but must also show the appropriateness in the LEA's proposal

7. Procrastination

Complaints

IDEA 2004 revises procedural safeguards to provide that LEAs, as well as parents, have the right to present complaints. Parties filing due process complaints must send a copy of the complaint to the other party as well as to the State agency. IDEA 2004 requires that in the case of a homeless child, the parent's notice of complaint to the LEA must contain the contact information for the child and the name of the school the child is attending.

A due process hearing is prohibited unless the requesting party has filed a complaint that meets specified notice requirements. SEAs are required to develop a model form to assist parents in filing due process complaint notices and complaints. Parents are required to receive the procedural safeguards notice generally only once a year but also upon: initial referral or parental request for an evaluation; a parent's registration of a due process complaint; or upon request by the parent.

IDEA 2004 allows an LEA to place a current copy of the procedural safeguards notice on its Internet website. The procedural safeguards must include notice to inform parents regarding specified matters, including time period in which parents may file complaints; the school district's opportunity to resolve a complaint before a due process hearing; and the time period in which a party can appeal a hearing officer's decision in court. A two-year timeline will be established for requesting a hearing on claims for reimbursed or ongoing compensatory education services, unless there is an applicable State timeline

Resolution

In order to try and facilitate resolution of conflict, IDEA 2004 provides that a parent may request mediation before filing a complaint and that mediation will be considered binding if both parties come to agreement. This written mediation agreement is enforceable in court. IDEA 2004 further authorizes a State agency to establish procedures to offer parents, as well as schools, that choose not to use the mediation process an opportunity to speak with a disinterested party regarding the benefits of mediation. IDEA 2004 provides for a resolution session to give parents and LEA's an opportunity to resolve the complaint before a due process hearing.

Hearing Officers

IDEA 2004 continues to require Hearing officers to make decisions on due process complaints based upon a determination of whether the child received a FAPE.

The law authorizes Hearing Officers, in matters alleging a procedural violation, to find that a child did not receive a FAPE only if the procedural inadequacies impeded the child's right to a FAPE; significantly impeded the parents' opportunity to participate in the decision-making process regarding FAPE provision; and or caused a deprivation of educational benefits.

I feel that you are violating my parental rights and in doing so you are also infringing upon my child's right to her federally mandated free and appropriate public education.

Chapter 10
Federal Monitoring

IDEA 2004 provides for monitoring, technical assistance, and enforcement of Part B programs. Directs the Secretary to:

- Monitor IDEA implementation through oversight of States' supervision and a system of performance indictors focused on improving educational results and functional outcomes for all children with disabilities.

- Enforce State compliance in making satisfactory progress toward improving educational results using certain indicators and benchmarks; and

- Require States to monitor and enforce LEA compliance. (U.S. Department of Education)

Requires the primary focus of Federal and State monitoring activities to be on improving educational results and functional outcomes for all children with disabilities, while ensuring compliance with program requirements. It also provides for various enforcement measures in cases of State needs for assistance, intervention, or substantial intervention.

IDEA 2004 sets the following monitoring priorities:

o   Provision for a FAPE in the least restrictive environment

o   State exercise of general supervisory authority;

and

o   Disproportionate representation of racial and ethnic groups in special education and related services, to the extent the overrepresentation is the result of inappropriate identification.

o   Requires States to develop State performance plans, including targets to measure progress in priority areas. (U.S. Department of Education)

The federal mandates also require SEA's to prohibit LEA's from reducing their efforts if they are not meeting IDEA part B requirements. State educational agencies can actually lose federal funding if it is determined that they are not found to be in compliance with the oversight of LEA's. So...if a LEA is not providing a FAPE for their students and the SEA is a) aware of the fact and b) chooses not to provide corrective action then both the LEA a SEA can lose federal funding. Now you see how a parent with the right information and ability to advocate effectively can wield significant power even when it doesn't feel that way as we sit in our little chairs at the meeting being "told" how our child will be served instead of included in the decision making process.

Legislative Impact

Under today's laws and policies, parents have more power and say in the education of their child. Parents have more rights, more involvement opportunity, and more decision-making authority than ever before. IDEA includes the provision: (7) Parent counseling and training means-

(i) Assisting parents in understanding the special needs of their child;

(ii) Providing parents with information about child development; and

(iii) Helping parents to acquire the necessary skills that will allow them to support the implementation of their child's IEP or IFSP.

NCLB includes rights, roles, and responsibilities that also offer parents and community leaders a strong voice in public education (*NCLB action guide). Parents may empower themselves with data and choices, utilizing school choice as a way to improve their child's educational opportunities. Choice empowers parents, but without training and understanding, parents and students may not benefit completely.

Policy Level Concerns

As involved parent advocates we should, as a group, be aware of and interested affecting policy in the areas of:

1. Increasing accountability and improving education results for students with disabilities.

2. Reducing the paperwork burden.

3. Improving early intervention strategies.

4. Reducing overidentification/misidentification of nondisabled children, including minority youth.

5. Encouraging innovative approaches to parental involvement and parental choice.

6. Supporting general education and special education teachers.

7. Rewarding innovation and improved education results.

8. Restoring trust and reducing litigation.

Conclusion

Wow. Seems overwhelming and it can very well be! However, with the right partnerships and supports any parent can be their child's best advocate. My time spent in education as a professional and as a parent (not to mention as a person with disabilities) has been a roller coaster of goods and not so goods. With enough parent involvement and communication with the schools, you can and will make a difference in the quality of services and supports your child receives! One thing I always remind the parents I work with is that my brother struggled with his own disabilities, again, undiagnosed. He is now a successful doctor with a wife and four beautiful children. The ultimate goal of this process is for your child to achieve a productive and fulfilling life as an adult beyond the scope of the school setting. It can be done!

The cost of special education is rising faster than that of regular education. Deciding the exact cost of special education is difficult as there are many types of general and special education supports a child may receive along with varying related services. The population in special education has also been rising faster than that of regular education. This information leads to the question; will cost cutting efforts be made at the expense of appropriate services to those in need? Although professionals claim to despise the idea of forcing parents into an advocacy role, the current budget crises and upheaval of educational systems, may indicate that more parent education is the only conceivable solution for a more appropriate education. Reading and using this handbook is a step towards this goal for yourself and your child.

Special education continues to be fraught with the bureaucratized process. In the 1997 reauthorization, the government promised to de-emphasize paperwork and process to focus on the needs of students. Instead the paperwork and bureaucratic processes increased tenfold. Yet is to be seen the impact of the new reauthorization. In order to truly effect change a more effective and proactive public education system will need to be implemented with parents aware and informed participating freely in their child's educational process. Making this brave step towards active involvement rather than passive involvement in your child's education is the key!

Children with disabilities and their families will need to have proactive and vocal advocacy networks to access and utilize as a support system. People who are actually willing to accompany a parent to an IEP or doctor's appointment, rather than giving them a website or phone number of a disembodied support "expert." Families in need or crisis need support rather than a bureaucratic route to follow up with. Without learning from the past, we are doomed to perpetuate failure on an even grander scale.

Family-school partnerships can serve as a foundation for positive change. Dr. Christenson with the National Association of School Psychologists said, "When students are having academic or behavioral difficulties at school, it is futile to debate whether the cause is at home, school, or elsewhere. Rather, it is helpful to identify contributing factors, especially the student's opportunity to learn at school and outside school, and how the assessment-intervention link empowers educators and parents in supporting the student to meet the task demands at school." Providing information, promoting open communication, and encouraging parents to pursue knowledge and training in their rights can be a step towards fostering partnerships. Some schools have previously hoarded the information and even discouraged professionals from providing parents with the sources for support. Seeking the information through books, websites, conferences and etc., allows you the parent to take control of receiving this crucial information.

In view of the issues facing parents of students with disabilities, the focus must remain that all children can learn and schools have the responsibility to teach them. School personnel and parents should work together in assuring a free appropriate education for all students. In order to truly empower parents, training and support must be provided. Programs should be well publicized and allow for easy access regardless of income. Good luck in your pursuit of a Free and Appropriate Public Education for your child!

> *The self is not something ready-made, but something in continuous formation through choice of action.*
>
> *-John Dewey*

TRAINING OPPORTUNITIES
PARENT TRAINING AND
INFORMATION CENTERS

Parent Training and Information Centers are designed to serve families of children with disabilities from birth to age 22. The centers work with families in obtaining appropriate education services and in training parents and professionals. Each state has at least one parent center. The centers help resolve conflicts between parents and other agencies or schools, and provide a connection for children with disabilities to the community resources needed. They assist in helping parents advocate effectively with professionals and agencies in meeting the educational needs of their children with disabilities (PTIC website, 2/24/04).

For more information go to: http://www.taalliance. org/centers/

GLOSSARY OF TERMS

Adequate yearly progress - Adequate yearly progress (AYP) is the minimum level of improvement that states, school districts, and schools must achieve each year. (U.S. Department of Education)

Assessments - Assessment is another word for "test." (U.S. Department of Education)

Classroom-based assessments - The most frequently used assessments are classroom tests prepared by teachers. These can take the form of brief, informal quizzes or more formal - midterms or final exams - and cover a longer period of class work.

Corrective action - When a school or school district does not make adequate yearly progress, the state will place it under a corrective action plan. The plan will include resources to improve teaching, administration or curriculum. If the school does not improve, then the state has increased authority to make any necessary, additional changes to ensure improvement. (U.S. Department of Education)

Disaggregated data - To disaggregate means to separate a whole into its parts. In education, this term means that test results are sorted by groups of students who are economically disadvantaged, from racial and ethnic minority groups, have disabilities, or have limited English fluency. This practice allows parents and teachers to see more than just the average score for their child's school. Instead, parents and teachers can see how each student group is performing. (U.S. Department of Education)

Elementary and Secondary Education Act (ESEA) - This is the primary federal law affecting K-12 education. It is also referred to as the No Child Left Behind (NCLB) Act, the name given to the law by the Bush administration when the law was reauthorized in January 2002. (U.S. Department of Education)

Family Educational Rights and Privacy Act (FERPA) - The Family Educational Rights and Privacy Act (FERPA) (20 U.S.C. § 1232g; 34 CFR Part 99) is a Federal law that protects the privacy of student education records. The law applies to all schools that receive funds under an applicable program of the U.S. Department of Education. FERPA gives parents certain rights with respect to their children's education records. These rights transfer to the student when he or she reaches the age of 18 or attends a school beyond the high school level. Students to whom the rights have transferred are "eligible students."

Free Appropriate Public Education (FAPE) - The term Free Appropriate Public Education (FAPE) is defined by law as:

Special education and related services which a) have been provided at public expense, under public supervision and direction, and without charge, b) meet the standards of the State education agency, c) include an appropriate pre-school, elementary, or secondary school education in the State involved, and

d) are provided in conformity with the individualized education program required under section (d). Section 602 P.L. 108-446

Highly qualified teacher - The new federal education law defines a "highly qualified teacher" as one who has obtained full state teacher certification or has passed the state teacher licensing examination and holds a license to teach in the state; holds a minimum of a bachelor's degree; and has demonstrated subject area competence in each of the academic subjects in which the teacher instructs. (NCLB)

Inclusion - Inclusion is the practice of placing students with disabilities in regular classrooms. Also known as mainstreaming. (NCEA)

Instruction - Instruction refers to the methods teachers use. Common methods are lecture, discussion, exercise, experiment, role-playing, small group, and writing assessments. The most effective teachers use many methods because not all are effective with all students. (NCEA)

Least Restrictive Environment - According to P.L. 108-446 Least Restrictive Environment means: school districts are required to educate students with disabilities in regular classrooms with their nondisabled peers, in the school they would attend if not disabled, to the maximum extent appropriate.

Local Education Agency (LEA) - According to the US Department of Education, a Local Education Agency (LEA) is a term used by the federal education law to describe a public board of education or other public authority within a state that maintains administrative control of public elementary or secondary schools in a city, county, school district, or other political subdivision.

Norm-referenced tests - The goal of these tests is to learn how students compare to each other by measuring their scores against an average national score. Norm-referenced tests are scored using a national curve in which half of the students receive a score above 50 percent and half below. The comparison group is called the "norm," explaining why these tests are generally comprised of multiple-choice and/or true-false questions.

Parental involvement - Parental involvement is the participation of parents in regular, two-way, meaningful communication involving students' academic learning and other school activities. The involvement includes ensuring that parents play an integral role in their child's learning; that parents are encouraged to be actively involved in their child's education at school; that parents are full partners in their child's education and are included, as appropriate, in decision making and on advisory committees. (NCLB)

School wide programs - School wide programs use Title I money to support comprehensive school improvement efforts and help all students, particularly low-achieving and at-risk students, meet state standards at particular schools. To qualify as a Title I school wide program, at least 40 percent of a school's students must be considered low-income. (Waivers can sometimes change the percentage.) School wide programs can provide Title I services and support to all of the children in the school, regardless of income level. School wide programs have more flexibility than targeted assistance programs when using Title I funds. For example, schools operating school wide programs can combine Title I funds with other federal, state, and local funding to finance a more comprehensive approach to improving student achievement. (U.S. Department of Education)

Scientifically based research - Research that involves the application of rigorous, systemic, and objective procedures to obtain reliable and valid knowledge relevant to educational activities/programs. (U.S. Department of Education)

State Education Agency (SEA) - A State Education Agency (SEA) is the agency under the federal education law, which is primarily responsible for supervising the state's public elementary and secondary schools.

Supplemental services - Students from low-income families who are attending schools that have been identified as "in need of school improvement" for two years will be eligible to receive outside tutoring or academic assistance. Parents can choose the appropriate services for their child from a list of approved providers. The school district will purchase the services. (U.S. Department of Education)

Title I - Title I is the name given to the first title of the federal No Child Left Behind (NCLB) Act. It provides federal funding for schools to help students who are behind academically or at risk of falling behind. Funding is based on the number of low-income children in a school, generally those eligible for the free lunch program. Title I is intended to supplement, not replace, state and district funds. Schools receiving Title I funds are supposed to involve parents in deciding how these funds are spent and in reviewing progress. (NCEA)

References

Chapter 1

Individuals with Disabilities Education Act 2004

Chapter 2

Macpherson, C.B. (1977). The Life and Times of Liberal Democracy. Oxford, New York: Oxford University Press, 2-75.

Sullivan, W.M. (1995). Work and Integrity The Crisis and Promise of Professionalism in America. New York: HarperBusiness A Division of HarperCollins*Publishers*, 33-34.

Tomas, A. & Grimes, J. (eds)(1995). Best practices in school psychology 3rd edition. Washington, DC: National Association of School Psychologists, 41 & 69.

Turnbull, H.R. & Turnbull, A., (2000). Free appropriate public education. Colorado: Love Publishing Company, 17, 31-34, 139.

Chapter 3

Americans With Disabilities Act Home Page website

Hallahan, D.P. & Kaufman, J.M., (1994). Exceptional children an introduction to special education 6th ed. Massachesetts: Allyn and Bacon, 41.

Jacob, S. & Hartshorne, T. (1991). Ethics and law for school psychologists. Vermont: Clinical Psychology Publishing Co., 31.

No Child Left Behind Act of 2001, 20 U.S.C.A.

Turnbull, H.R. & Turnbull, A., (2000). Free appropriate public education. Colorado: Love Publishing Company, 17, 31-34, 139.

Turnbull, H.R. & Turnbull, A., Shank, M., Smith, S. & Leal, D. (2002). Exceptional Lives Special Education in Today's Schools (3rd ed.). Upper Saddle River, New Jersey: Merrill Prenctice Hall.

Chapter 4

Lane, K.E., Connelly, M.J., Mead, J.F., Gooden, M.A., & Eckes (Eds.). (2005). The Principal's Legal Handbook (3rd ed.). Dayton, Ohio: Education Law Association.

LexisNexis Editorial Staff. (2005), IDEA Reauthorized 2004 Amendments to the Individuals with Disablities Education Act. Charlottesville, VA: Matthew Bender & Company, Inc., a member of the LexisNexis Group.

Turnbull, H.R. & Turnbull, A., (2000). Free appropriate public education. Colorado: Love Publishing Company, 17, 31-34, 139.

CHAPTER 8

Canter, A.S. (1997). The future of intelligence testing in the schools. *School Psychology Review,* 26, 255-261.

Elliott, S.N., & Fuchs, L.S. (1997). The utility of curriculum-based measurement and performance assessment as alternatives to traditional intelligence and achievement tests. *School Psychology Review,* 26, 224-233.

Fuchs, L.S., Fuchs, D., & Speece, D.L., (2002). Treatment validity as a unifying construct for identifying learning disabilities. *Learning Disabilities Quarterly,* 25, 33-45.

Fuchs, D., Mock, D., Morgan, P.L., & Young, C.L., (2003). Responsiveness-to-Intervention: Definitions, evidence, and implications for the learning disabilities construct. *Learning Disabilities Research & Practice,* 18, 157-171

Marston, D., Muyskens, P., Lau, M., & Canter, A. (2003). Problem-solving model for decision making with high-incidence disabilities: The Minneapolis experience. *Learning Disabilities Research & Practice,* 18, 187-200.

Sattler, J. M. (1992). Assessment of children revised and updated 3rd edition. San Diego: Jerome M. Sattler, Publisher, Inc., 5-14.

Schinn, M.R.(ed) (1989). Curriculum-Based Measurement Assessing Special Children. New York: The Guilford Press, 18-71.

Tomas, A. & Grimes, J. (eds)(1995). Best practices in school psychology 3rd edition. Washington, DC: National Association of School Psychologists, 41 & 69.

Turnbull, H.R. & Turnbull, A., (2000). Free appropriate public education. Colorado: Love Publishing Company, 17, 31-34, 139.

Vaughn, S. & Fuchs, L., (2003). Redefining learning disabilities as inadequate response to instruction: The promise and potential problems. *Learning Disabilities Research & Practice,* 18, 137-146.

Chapter 10

U.S. Department of Education website

No Child Left Behind Act of 2001, 20 U.S.C.A.

General References:

Braden, J.P. & Kratochwill, T.R., (1997). Treatment utility of assessment: Myths and realities. *School Psychology Review*, 26, 475-485.

Canter, A.S. (1997). The future of intelligence testing in the schools. *School Psychology Review*, 26, 255-261.

Elliott, S.N., & Fuchs, L.S. (1997). The utility of curriculum-based measurement and performance assessment as alternatives to traditional intelligence and achievement tests. *School Psychology Review*, 26, 224-233.

Fuchs, L.S., Fuchs, D., & Speece, D.L., (2002). Treatment validity as a unifying construct for identifying learning disabilities. *Learning Disabilities Quarterly,*25, 33-45.

Fuchs, D., Mock, D., Morgan, P.L., & Young, C.L., (2003). Responsiveness-to-Intervention: Definitions, evidence, and implications for the learning disabilities construct. *Learning Disabilities Research & Practice*, 18, 157-171.

Hallahan, D.P. & Kaufman, J.M., (1994). Exceptional children an introduction to special education 6th ed. Massachesetts: Allyn and Bacon, 41.

Harrison, K., (2003) Understanding Professionalism in Education, 2003, p.35.

Jacob, S. & Hartshorne, T. (1991). Ethics and Law for School Psychologists. Vermont: Clinical Psychology Publishing Co., 31.

Lane, K.E., Connelly, M.J., Mead, J.F., Gooden, M.A., & Eckes (Eds.). (2005). The Principal's Legal Handbook (3rd ed.). Dayton, Ohio: Education Law Association.

LexisNexis Editorial Staff. (2005), IDEA Reauthorized 2004 Amendments to the Individuals with Disablities Education Act. Charlottesville, VA: Matthew Bender & Company, Inc., a member of the LexisNexis Group.

Marston, D., Muyskens, P., Lau, M., & Canter, A. (2003). Problem-solving model for decision making with high-incidence disabilities: The Minneapolis experience. *Learning Disabilities Research & Practice,* 18, 187-200.

Macpherson, C.B. (1977). The Life and Times of Liberal Democracy. Oxford, New York: Oxford University Press, 2-75.

Nealis, L.K. (2004). IDEA and NCLB: Get you facts straight at convention.

Communiqué NASP, March 2004.

No Child Left Behind Act of 2001, 20 U.S.C.A.

Sattler, J. M. (1992). Assessment of children revised and updated 3rd edition. San Diego: Jerome M. Sattler, Publisher, Inc., 5-14.

Tomas, A. & Grimes, J. (eds)(1995). Best practices in school psychology 3rd edition. Washington, DC: National Association of School Psychologists, 41 & 69.

Turnbull, H.R. & Turnbull, A., (2000). Free appropriate public education. Colorado: Love Publishing Company, 17, 31-34, 139.

Turnbull, H.R. & Turnbull, A., Shank, M., Smith, S. & Leal, D. (2002). Exceptional Lives Special Education in Today's Schools (3rd ed.). Upper Saddle River, New Jersey: Merrill Prenctice Hall.

Vaughn, S. & Fuchs, L., (2003). Redefining learning disabilities as inadequate response to instruction: The promise and potential problems. *Learning Disabilities Research & Practice,* 18, 137-146.

NOTES:

1790940

Made in the USA